D1768564

The God Hunt

A Discovery Book
for Men and Women

David and Karen Mains

David C. Cook Publishing Co.

4

David C. Cook Publishing Co., Elgin, Illinois 60120
David C. Cook Publishing Co., Weston, Ontario
THE GOD HUNT—A DISCOVERY BOOK FOR MEN AND WOMEN

Designed by Britt Taylor Collins
First Printing, 1984
Printed in the United States of America
89 88 87 86 85 84   5 4 3 2 1

Library of Congress Cataloging in Publication Data
Mains, David R.
   The God hunt.
   1. Christian life—1960-   . 2. Mains, David R.
3. Mains, Karen Burton.   I. Mains, Karen Burton.
II. Title.
BV4501.2.M3265   1984   248.4   84-12674
ISBN 0-89191-813-2

Contents

1
THE GOD HUNT

Karen:

I lost my husband once in a motel in Fort Wayne, Indiana.

The first one dressed that morning, I headed out early to find the free coffee the management advertised. After filling two Styrofoam cups, I cautiously made my way down one hall, negotiated a left turn without mishap, and inched down another long, long corridor with my eyes glued to the sloshing coffee. Glancing up, I looked at the long row of identical doors—and had absolutely no clue as to which room was ours!

These minor comedies of the absurd make up much of my life. One door matched another door which matched another door and stretched to the exit sign at the end of the hallway. Here was a visual symbol of life and infinity. And I was lost in this eternity, immobilized by two sloshing coffee cups and a bad memory for numbers.

Calling, "David . . . David . . . David?" was obviously out of the question, and I knew better than to think he would eventually come looking for me. I am a woman of independent emotional means; my husband *counts* on me to take care of myself. Navigating back to the lobby for room information was also undesirable. I would never make it that far and return without spilling the coffee.

Just stand here a moment and be quiet, I thought. Surely my trusty, subjective mind (which has bailed me out of many awkward circumstances) would soon toss up the room number I had forgotten. Then, a minor miracle put an end to my minor dilemma. I heard David blowing his nose behind one of those doors. After twenty-two years of marriage (that's forty-four seasons of hay fever, both spring and fall), I have become utterly familiar with the sound of David's nose blowing. I knew which was the right room.

This mundane incident is a perfect illustration of the way we hear the word of the Lord spoken to our inner heart.

When we're standing in a long corridor with a confusing number of doors, unable to knock or run because we're stuck with these two steaming cups of coffee, we recognize that familiar sound. We recognize it because we have deliberately cultivated an enduring, intimate relationship over the years.

Nor does one have to be married to understand this kind of intimacy. A phone rings. There is no face or form to identify the caller, but we hear a voice and know who is calling. It is the voice of one we love. Or we are in a crowded room and can scarcely see the faces, but someone laughs and our soul is warmed. A favorite friend is near.

I've read that telephone technology soon will recognize individual voiceprints. A screening device will monitor incoming calls and throw the switch to the coffeepot or stove when the right voice phones. A microphone at the door will transmit a voice pattern to the phone which will unlock the front door.

When we hear the familiar voice of a friend, we know who it is. There is a voiceprint on our hearts. After years of intimacy, the same is true of God. His voiceprint is on our souls, and we recognize his divine whispers.

But how does the average, ordinary Christian learn to recognize this voice? By establishing the discipline of identifying God in our everyday world.

For David and me this has meant going on what we call the God Hunt. What is the God Hunt? It's any time when God works in or touches our daily world *and we recognize it to be him.*

In the Mains family, this pursuit takes the form of a spiritual game. Let me illustrate with an example from "Sighting Day," a story in our book,

*Tales of the Kingdom.** In this story, the children of Great Park attempt to sight the King who appears in disguises. As soon as they make a Sighting, they go to the practice field where they spend the afternoon playing with the King. Hero (the reluctant hero of these tales) is perturbed because he never sees the King.

"Why can my brother see the King when I can't?" he asks a young man (who really is the King in disguise).

The young man answers, "Your brother can see the King because he is a little child, and little children play the game best of all. The others see the King because they believe and have been given the gift of seeing. Here, in the park, believing comes before seeing."

Hero spends the afternoon enjoying games with the other children and with the young man, and finally that evening—definitely come-lately—he cries, "I see the King!"

After I read this story at a mother/daughter retreat and explained its scriptural truth, little girls from nine years old to grandmas of eighty were making "Sightings" all weekend. Children of all ages can play this spiritual game.

The Westminster Shorter Catechism states that the chief end of man is to glorify God and to *enjoy* him. Often we do not identify God in our everyday world because we look for him with an adult's analytic rationality. Christ's instructions are particularly applicable here: "Let the little children come to Me, and do not forbid them; for of such is the kingdom of God. Assuredly, I say to you, whoever does not receive the kingdom of God as a little child will by no means enter it" (Luke 18:16,17, NKJ).

Children have a great capacity for delight and for wonder. They easily suspend the rational and accept the improbable. Not that seeing God in our everyday world is a nonrational activity. But we can best identify the supernatural in the commonplace when we approach it with the attitude we held when we played hide-and-seek.

Remember the blindfolded eyes and the hiding. Remember the hunt. Remember the rustle in the bushes, the muffled cough, the instinct for finding a hidden play companion. Remember the delicious excitement when creeping close to the hidden quarry. That is the exact feeling of childlike anticipation we want to capture as we set out on the God Hunt.

*David and Karen Mains, *Tales of the Kingdom* (David C. Cook, 1983).

Although God is always there, I sometimes have the feeling that he hides so we will come seeking him. I am also certain that he takes delight in our surprise, and in a sense, he jumps out from his hiding place and shouts, "Boo!"

One of the most beautiful sounds in the world is that of children collapsing in delirious laughter. I love to hear my children laughing. In the same way, God loves the delighted, spiritual laughter that comes when his children find him in their everyday world.

Jeremiah 29:13, 14 invites us to play this game, "And you will seek Me and find Me, when you search for Me with all your heart. I will be found by you" (NKJ).

We cannot play this spiritual game passively. We must go on the hunt. We must enter into it actively. In hide-and-seek, the seeker must go seeking, or if he stays close to "home," he at least keeps his eyes and ears open.

When David and I experience God in our everyday world and recognize that it is indeed he, we call out "I spy." Even a child can learn to make these spiritual sightings. Our eleven-year-old, the youngest of our four, came home from school recently and reported, "I had three 'I spys' today."

One of the prayers we prayed for Jeremy at the beginning of the school year was that he would make good friends. Highly motivated creatively, Jeremy designed a game which soon occupied eleven of his classmates who traipsed in and out of the house over a period of months. Jeremy suddenly had friends in abundance, and many of his "I spys" were related to this answered prayer.

When Adam and Eve walked with God in the garden, their relationship with him was experiential, and it was severed when they fell from innocence. The work of Christ is to restore that relationship with our Creator. The power of the Holy Spirit renews sight to our blinded spiritual eyes so that we may see the King who walks among us in disguise, so that we might all *spy* God *every day.*

This work of restoration renews innocence and reawakens a spiritual childlikeness. We pray that you will begin the daily pursuit of the God who is there and identify his activity in your everyday life.

Then when you stand outside that long corridor of closed doors, confused as to where you belong, having lost the memory of the right number, juggling your awkward responsibilities, and you hear a familiar, well-loved sound behind one of the doors, you will know it is God who is present. There is the door you are to push open. This is the way and the right number. Here is the place where you are to enter and to stay.

Your Turn:
BEGINNING THE HUNT

Karen:

While driving down a country road, a friend cried, "Oh, stop! There's bittersweet!" It was only when she pointed out the vines intertwined in the branches of the trees that I could see them. Then I wondered how I could have missed the obvious touches of color in the late fall landscape.

My friend spotted the bright orange berries because she knew what she was looking for. She had trained her eye to see the beauty in the natural world, and she gathered the weeds and pods for lovely wreaths and arrangements. This visual keenness allowed her to see what other people could not.

We always find what we are looking for. When I was pregnant with each of our four children, it seemed as if the world was filled with other pregnant women! Our oldest son is an amateur ornithologist, and his eye spots birds on telephone wires or in soaring patterns that I never notice. David tells me how comfortable he is becoming with middle age; now that he is going grey, the world seems filled with other mid-life, grey-haired men.

The same principle works when we are looking for God. Once the hunt truly begins, we see evidences of his Presence in all of life. We prayed, and a life was spared. There was no money, and an unexpected check came in the mail. We begin to see a pattern and think "God has walked in this place today."

Begin the God Hunt by looking back. Attempt to remember the times when you were convinced you had found evidence of God's presence. The supernatural encounter was startlingly real at the time. A miraculous healing took place in your extended family that people talk about to this day. You recall religious meetings where the room was filled with the power of the Holy Spirit.

Begin by thinking: *When I was a child, were there any times when I sensed that God was near to me?* Quickly jot down enough details to make the memory clear, and continue through the other stages of your life.

CHILDHOOD

ADOLESCENCE

Sample
The English teacher who wrote across one of my papers, "You have a gift for writing," was used by God to influence my entire future. *Karen Mains*

EARLY ADULT YEARS

Sample

The broken romance in college was used by God to delay me until my future (and younger) wife would have a chance to grow up and be ready for marriage. *David Mains*

MIDDLE ADULT YEARS

LATE ADULT YEARS

"The impulse to pursue God originates with God, but the outworking of that impulse is our following hard after him, and all the time we are already in his hand: 'Thy right hand upholdeth me.'"

A.W. Tozer
The Pursuit of God

But how does the average, ordinary Christian learn to recognize this voice? By establishing the discipline of identifying God in our everyday world.

2
HINDRANCES TO THE HUNT

David:

Why are so many of us like Hero, unable to see the King? One reason we do not "see" the supernatural world that surrounds us is that many Christians have begun to think with the same secular world view as the culture in which they live. They have become what I call "secularized Christians," and secular thinking always blindfolds the eyes of the inner spiritual person.

Karen wrote a short satire for our "Chapel of the Air" broadcast which illustrates how this happens. It parodies the type of overblown reporting which takes itself a little too seriously and might be read in the Arts and Literary section of any national magazine.

Karen:

Winchell Gstaadt's trouble began when he decided to paint the night, or as the *Newark Canvas and Sculpture Review* quoted him (April 1983), "to really paint the night, to paint it totally as it has never before been painted."

Tome magazine dubbed Winchell the "art child of this age" and featured his face on the cover and his works in a twelve-page spread. *The Artiste* lauded Gstaadt's "edginess," or his ability, despite frequent critical dismay, to be always on the advance edge of what is soon to become popularly acclaimed.

Gstaadt approached painting by first immersing himself in his subject, sometimes for weeks or for months or even years on end. If he was painting flowers (as he did during the decade of the '60s), he would move into a nearby botonarium (upon permission of a local park district or academic science department) and "live and breathe and feel the essence of flower."

"I exult" quoted *Harlequin University's Quarterly Review*, "in the naturalness of the growing environs, in the soilishness of being planted and rooted, in the florid delicacy of blooming. My very blood stimulates chlorophyll. My heart begins to beat in synch with osmosis. This, then is what I paint, this intimate identification I have come to know, not the objective reality I see" (Winter Quarter 1964).

The first canvases to emerge from Winchell's night period (which began in 1980 and, tragically, may never end) were wild streaks of cobalt brushed with dazzling blotches of starlike bursts of fire, but as the artist more and more pursued his "essence of experience," the canvases became reduced in size and darker.

This "essence of experience" demanded much of Gstaadt. He began to work from sunset to sunrise. "The night! The night!" his housekeeper heard him frequently exclaim. Soon he demanded that all his meals be served in the planetarium he had constructed on the back forty of his restored Connecticut farm.

In the last interview in *Gamechild,* conducted by cultural editor Garson L. Greystone, Gstaadt declared that he was attempting to capture "that moment of chaos before creation when nothingness was everything, when the heart of the creator (small c—everyman) was in absolute blackness."

According to Fern Farmer (Gstaadt's faithful gardener), the artist would sit in the night for hours, "Jes' doin' nothin'. Jes' sittin' there, gettin' the essence. Yep. Gettin' the essence." Then Winchell began spending hours outside at night, walking his fields and wearing sunglasses in the dark. Finally, he pulled a J. L. Breen ragwool cap over his head. Over this he tied a blindfold.

The canvases resulting from this period of immersion were absolutely black. Gstaadt also sprayed three dimensional objects (the kinds of things one bumps into in the dark) with a house paint called "Midnight."

These were titled "Assemblage Black #1," "Assemblage Black #2," etc.

"It's dark here," declared Gstaadt one morning. "Really, totally, dark. No light. No stars. Nothing." Upon examination, Gstaadt's doctors discovered that the artist could no longer see.

"A form of psychological blindness resulting from intense emotional identification," explained Gstaadt's longtime friend and therapist, Armand Char, M.D. "It's a good thing this didn't happen to Winnie during his flower period."

So the great modern artist, Winchell Gstaadt, that prophet of the contemporary artistic wave, is blind. There is no light in his night, nor in his day either. The psychiatrists attending his case are mum about his prognosis and there's no comment from the artist who has gone into seclusion in his planetarium.

The gardener Farmer seems to have the only, and therefore last, word about his employer, "I jes' guess he got the essence of it. Yup."

David:

Poor Winchell Gstaadt, a fictional friend but a fitting illustration of today's secular man and woman. Deliberately blindfolding his eyes, he walks the fields of the world refusing to see the light to prove some obscure point about identification; but that intense association has left Gstaadt functionally blind. So it is with the secularized person who has chosen not to see the Light that shines in this world's night. Clinging to pet ideas, he pulls a hat over his head and refuses to notice, "Hey! Those really are stars up there!"

The prophets, those grizzled old nuisances, aptly described this current phenomenon many hundreds of years ago. Pointing fingers and generally making fools of themselves, they cried, "You have eyes to see and do not see. . . ." They knew then as today's true (and equally pesty) prophets know now: *The human is always in danger of losing the inward sight of the soul, of being spiritually blind.*

Secular. We use the word frequently, but what does it mean? *Webster's New Unabridged Dictionary* gives us a definition: "Pertaining to the world or to things not spiritual and sacred; relating to or connected with worldly things; disassociated from religious teaching or principles; worldly; as *secular* education, *secular* music."

The Apostle John, that wide-eyed visionary for whom the spiritual was the whole, defined secularism for the first-century church: "Beloved . . . test the spirits, whether they are of God. . . . Every spirit that confesses that Jesus Christ has come in the flesh is of God, and every spirit that does not confess that Jesus Christ has come in the flesh is not of God" (I John 4:1-3 NKJ).

So? The church has always lived in a secular world. The church will take the high road and the world will take the low road and never the twain shall meet. Right?

Wrong! When the majority of a population, including the thought influencers, turns away from the God of Life and chooses to walk in the darkness, Death begins foot stomping on all of us with a variety of violent dance steps.

I have never attended an X-rated movie, but I often gasp in horror at the suffocating tales of X-rated life that come through pastoral counseling. During counseling, I was horrified to hear of a witches' coven that practiced infant sacrifice in a nearby midwestern community.

But why am I surprised? A sacrifice of the innocents is going on in our culture which is proportionate to the rise of the death dance of secularism. Daily newspapers give detailed accounts of little children being tortured to death by a parent. The raping of male and female children by close relatives is epidemic. Children are used for sexual subjects in hardcore pornographic photographs and films.

Where is the altar? It seems to be all over the land. In nearly any home. In front of any TV set where the ritualistic practice ceremonies are enacted. Anywhere in the darkness.

But not in Christian homes. Right?

A therapist friend shared recently, "I'm appalled by the abusiveness I find in the Christian men I'm counseling."

"What kind of abuse?" I was almost afraid to ask.

He raised his hands in despair. "All kinds of abuse. Verbal. Emotional. Physical. There's one pastor in town who I'm convinced hates children. And these men have such incredible denial. They think they're not abusive because they're not as bad as their fathers. 'I'm not like my father,' they say. But there is only one standard. *Only one.* It is Jesus Christ. How would *he* behave? How would he treat my wife? How would he treat my child? Christ is the *only* standard."

I knew my friend's indignation. I also have counseled with the victims who have been offered on the altar of this world. "My mother beat me mercilessly with a coat hanger." "A youth pastor raped my daughter." "My husband abuses me—I don't know how to stop him." And most of the stories I hear are within the context of the church. Something is happening to *our* thinking. We are assimilating the viewpoint of the world around us, and we don't even recognize it.

John identifies the God of this world. "Every spirit that does not confess that Jesus Christ has come in the flesh is not of God. And this is the *spirit* of the Antichrist, which you have heard was coming, and is now already in the world" (I John 4:3 NKJ).

Note that John is talking about an attitude, not a person—the *spirit* of antichrist, not *the* Antichrist. This is the pervasive attitude which states that Jesus is not the Christ. It is a system of doctrines and practices that rejects any form of religious faith and worship. This attitude is building the platform, constructing the scaffolding, placing chairs for dignitaries, raising the placards, and drawing the crowd which will eventually shout "Heil!" to that one against whose coming the Scriptures issue dire warning.

Yet the saddest truth of all seems to be: *Most Christians fail at living as true Christians in a secular world.*

We become secularized Christians, a contradiction in terms. We don't walk in the light; we walk in the half-light. We hold vigorously to the forms of Christianity—a weekly Bible study group, church on Sunday morning, grace before family meals, five sleepy minutes in the evening for Bible reading—but we really function in alignment with the spirit of our age. For instance, we abuse our children, either through neglect or out of the hatred in our hearts, and we are proud that we are not "like our fathers."

Blinded, we cannot see that we are bowing at the world's altars. The true standard for behavior is Christ, but we cannot see him because we walk in the darkness of this world. It's dark out there. There is no Light.

The family cat died in Karen's study two days ago. She was a little grey cat our daughter Melissa brought home years ago, and she delivered endless litters which she birthed in bathtubs or boxes in the garage.

After Karen arranged for our veterinarian to put an end to Maisie's tri-annual litters, the cat was never quite the same. Becoming thin and mopey, she slept a lot. Suddenly she began to die, curled on the end of the sofa in my wife's office—her favorite soft and warm place in the house.

"Your room smells bad," I said to Karen this morning. She flared, then apologized, and explained, "It's just that I'm so tired of the stink of death."

I knew she was referring to the stink of death in the world as well as that of a loved family pet. No apologies were needed, because I, too, am tired of the stink of death. I am weary with a culture that is dying and doesn't know it is in the death throes, of a corporate church that mistakes the odor of funeral for incense. I am appalled by Christians who have pulled the ragwool cap over their blindfolded eyes and stand in the night and sing hymns but never see God.

There's a little bit of Winchell Gstaadt in every Christian, and a lot of him in more than some.

Let us beware of the spiritual blindness caused by intense emotional identification with the spirit of our world.

Your Turn:
DRAW YOUR OWN CONCLUSIONS

David:

One way to determine how secularized our thinking has become is to evaluate the daily influences which touch our lives, but which we seldom consider detrimental. The following self evaluation lists fifteen categories. Fill in at least ten of these with your own examples:

Fill out at least ten of these fifteen categories.

1. News magazine most often read

2. Favorite media talk show (nonreligious)

3. Advertiser whose direct mail I normally examine

4. Entertainment series watched regularly on TV

5. Nonreligious cause with which I identify

6. Favorite actor or actress

7. Newspaper most often read

8. Popular music group or artist I like

9. Favorite comic strip

10. A respected political personality

11. Company with commercials I enjoy

12. An admired sports figure

13. Sports, home, or fashion magazine read often

14. Most listened-to radio or TV news show

15. A favorite nonreligious writer

Christian	Neutral	Reflects Spirit of Antichrist	Blatantly Antichrist

Now draw your own conclusions. Evaluate as best you can the mind-set behind each item. Use John's definition—"Every spirit that does not confess that Jesus Christ has come in the flesh is not of God"—to determine the world view which you think best describes each of your examples. Is it Christian? (*Christianity Today* obviously affirms that Christ is Lord. You might not agree with every article in this magazine, but its basic editorial mind-set is to uphold Christ and his Kingdom.) Is it neutral? (*National Geographic* obviously celebrates the created world, but when it assumes that creation is not related to a deistic mind and sustained divine plan, then perhaps its approach is mixed. The subscribing Christian needs to inform himself of this scientific mind-set.)

Does it reflect the spirit of antichrist? (Does the movie we have just seen uphold violence and denigrate traditional Christian values? Is Christ's name continually taken in vain? Is there a bias which affirms that sex outside of marriage is preferable?) Is it blatantly antichrist? (Does it openly proclaim godlessness? Does it overtly stand against the teachings of Christ?)

The watershed question is: What is the author's or editor's or producer's mind-set toward Christ? This is a consciousness-raising exercise. It is not designed so that you can withdraw from everything in your world which is not outright Christian; it is intended to make you more sensitive to the influencers in our society. When you read or view them, you can remind yourself from which thought system they came. This knowledge is in itself a protection against subtle secularization of the Christian's thoughts. It is one more step in preparing to go on the God Hunt.

Secularism: "A secular spirit, views, or the like; especially, a system of doctrines and practices that rejects any form of religious faith and worship."
Webster's New Unabridged Dictionary

3
MAKING SIGHTINGS

Karen:

This fall my oldest son and I stole a day together. We headed toward a wildlife sanctuary in Wisconsin where Canada geese water on their migratory flights. Since on this visit the migratory activity was quiet, Randall and I took to the trails and attempted to make other bird sightings.

I love to go birding with my son because he is a serious ornithologist who is rarely far from a pair of binoculars or a field guide. Randall's identification ability amazes me. (He spotted deer frozen in protective stillness in the brush that I overlooked only fifteen feet away.) His eye has become so developed he can tell the species of a bird by the shape of its tail in flight, by its unique soaring patterns, or even by my inadequate descriptions over the phone.

Outside my bedroom window is the "bird tree." Here the birds stack up in landing patterns as they wait to feed at the feeders which hang outside the first-floor windows. Often while talking on the phone, I watch the chickadees and downy woodpeckers and nuthatches crack open the sunflower seeds they have gathered. Frequently, I interrupt conversations with Randall to say, "Oh, there's the most unusual little yellow bird with black breast stripes, the size of a finch but not a finch."

"That's a magnolia warbler," Randall will inform me. "They're migrating. If you look around, you'll probably see others since they usually migrate in groups." And as I look, I discover a variety of little birds with variation of coloring, and I feel privileged that they have chosen our trees and feeders for resting from their spring flight.

Like all good ornithologists, Randall keeps a life identification list. There are about nine thousand species of birds in the world, and this feathered treasure hunt goes on for the bird lover as long as he or she lives.

Not only is my son finding what he is looking for, he is opening my eyes to the beauty of these creatures. Now when my soul is weary, I watch the birds feed and take delight in the bright patchwork of blue jay, red cardinal, and herringbone woodpecker.

Going on the God Hunt is much like being serious about ornithology. We take a field guide and a good pair of binoculars and walk out into the world to watch for God. When making God Sightings, our field guide is Scripture, which points out the intrinsic details of the nature of God. Thus and so does he act; this is how to identify the supernatural which coexists with the natural world. Prayer is the illuminator, the binoculars that magnify the vision of the inward eyes.

David and I also keep "life lists." We have formed a habit of writing down our different Sightings. This discipline heightens the inward eye's ability to see God. We can catch the quick flight of the supernatural wings or hear the high morning call and know it is he. We can tell by the soaring pattern that the Divine Eagle is watching high above. This feather dropped on our path is a reminder of his presence.

Again, the God Hunt is any time God intervenes or works in our everyday world, and we recognize it to be him.

We have chosen four specific areas in which to distinguish the activity of God. While we are well aware that God can convey himself to our world by any means he chooses, these four categories are helpful to the novice hunter.

The categories are:
— Any obvious answer to prayer.
— Any unexpected evidence of God's care.
— Any help to do God's work in the world.
— Any unusual linkage or timing.

Because David and I have developed the discipline of keeping prayer journals, we have a record of our Sightings. As we pray, we write down our requests. When a prayer is answered, we jot the date and a few details or comments in a column beside the specific request.

One or two incidents of seemingly answered prayers might be called coincidences, but the cumulative evidence of thirteen years of answered prayer, all recorded in journals, becomes weighty in its cumulative effect. It would be next to impossible to convince me that God doesn't answer prayer. I have personal and satisfactory evidence to the contrary.

An illustration of *answered prayer* took an unexpected turn this summer. I had promised to speak to a group of six hundred pastors' wives with great reluctance because my schedule at that time was forbidding. The younger boys, David, and I had been involved in a Christian conference on the west coast for a week, spent a half week in transit (on Amtrak), and returned home for a week when I had five broadcasts to write and record. Sometime during the week I had to get the four of us ready to drive to another conference in North Carolina.

The morning that I spoke to the pastors' wives my prayer journal entry said, "Lord, help me to get a decent dinner on the table this evening." Everyone was planning to be home for the evening meal, and I had heard some rather vociferous complaints about my tendency to use short-order foods in times of busyness.

My speaking topic was "Who Takes Care of the Caretakers?" When I finished, two young women came to me and said, "Our husbands are occupied all afternoon, and we really don't have anything we must do. Is there something we could do to take care of *you?*"

They came home with me and whipped together a wonderful dinner while I finished writing a broadcast. That next day when I read my prayer requests I wrote, "God, you are something else!" He used two pastor's wives from New York to feed the hungry (for good food) family of a radio minister in Illinois. I spy!

A dramatic illustration of God's *unexpected care* took place in one of the life-preservation incidents which seem to occur so often in our family. David had also accepted an invitation to speak at a conference on the east coast. Because he wanted to take the two younger boys with him, he decided to drive. Then he invited my seven-year-old nephew to come along, thinking it might as well be a special event for as many as possible.

The first leg of the journey was a night drive. David was suddenly startled by what sounded like an explosion. The whole back window of the station wagon had been shattered by who knows what—a rock? a bullet? David was very aware that our nephew Brendon had been pressing his face to that window only moments before. He had moved away, and no one was hurt. God's unexpected care was just a matter of a few seconds. (Sighting! Something else for the life list.)

Even when accidents *are* involved, our inner eye sees God's protective hand *because we have developed the habit of looking for God.*

Driving home with two of the children late one afternoon, I stopped behind a car waiting to make a left turn. Traffic was heavy, and the peculiar sunset light made it hard to notice red brake lights. A young woman driving behind me braked, swerved, sideswiped our car, and plowed into the rear end of the car stopped ahead of us.

The older couple in the first car was stunned, but none of us sustained any injuries. I was immediately filled with a sense of my God's protective presence. Imagine what might have happened if we had been hit directly by a car going fifty miles per hour with another car in front of us.

Because I was aware of God's care, I was supernaturally empowered to minister love. A woman in "The Chapel of the Air" office later finished this tale for me. A friend of hers knew the couple in the first car and knew that I had been involved in the accident. When they commented to him on how kind I had been, he explained that I was a Christian.

David and I have countless illustrations of this category—*any help to do God's work in the world.* We are convinced daily that we couldn't keep the broadcast, writing, speaking, or personal ministries of our lives going without Divine intervention. David is putting a broadcast together, the time for recording it is coming close, and someone puts an article in his hand that is exactly what he needs to tie the entire thrust together in a powerful manner.

I've spent a day in the kitchen cooking my favorite recipes, and I just "happen" to stick several extra casseroles in the freezer. Someone I love experiences tragedy, and I am able to express that love in a tangible way by my already prepared gift of food.

An illustration of *unusual linkage or timing* involved our two older children, both college students. I have always had difficulty establishing the discipline of fasting. In fact, this exercise has not been a frequent one in the spiritual profile of our family. Recently David was away on a two-week teaching trip among pastors in India. Randall, our oldest child, mentioned that he had been fasting for his father and was learning much through this effort.

"Ha!" I thought. "If my own child can fast, I ought to be able to stick with it myself!" That was the impetus I needed, and I was able to maintain a couple days of full fasting as well as keep a week of one-meal-a-day fasting.

During this time I talked to our daughter who was at college near Boston. She mentioned that she had been fasting and was experiencing an unusual sense of God's presence. Neither Randy nor I had told her of our experience with the discipline.

Then I received an international phone call from David in Cochin, India. There had been a great moving of God in the meetings, and David was weeping so that he could scarcely convey this wonderful message to me. As we compared notes after he returned home, we discovered that he also had been led to fast for a day.

Linkage, timing. Only God could have worked this amazing spiritual exercise in the network of our family life. He united us on a spiritual front so that he could use our prayers in a special work in India!

David often talks about the "naturalness" of the supernatural, how supernatural surprises are most often garmented in the ordinary.

Without a doubt, much of this generation is a glutton for miracles. We prefer the supernatural to invade our world magically. We want the natural laws of order suspended. We want the bush to flame and refuse to recognize it if it just rustles. If God does not show himself—poof! boom! bah!—accompanied by a puff of smoke, then he is not God enough, we think.

Consequently we miss the greater miracle, that God fills all of life. He makes the ordinary holy with his presence. He hides himself in the crux of the everyday moment. He is intimate. And we can walk with him in the garden among the slugs and the hot sun and the soil, among the vegetables as well as the flowers. Wherever we are growing spiritually,

God is there in the naturalness of the supernatural.

Your Turn:
MAKING REQUESTS

David:

Why don't we make more God Sightings in answered prayer than we do? Sometimes we've forgotten what we prayed for by the time we receive the answer. One solution to this is keeping a list of our requests—the simplest form of a prayer journal.

Another reason is that we don't think before we pray. I find it helpful to ask myself six simple questions when making requests of God. Try using them to organize your thoughts before praying.

1. *What specifically do I want?* Many prayer requests are so general it is impossible to tell whether or not God has answered them. "Bless Aunt Sally." "Bless the missionaries." What do we mean by this? And how will we know when the bless-'em prayers are answered? We need to learn to be specific. "Help Aunt Sally to overcome her fear of aging. Grant our missionary friends strength for spiritual battles and physical strength to combat fatigue."

2. *Can God grant such a request?* God is all-powerful, yet he chooses to limit himself to the natural laws which he created. He also will not violate the gift of free will which he has given to all people. "Make so-and-so do such-and-such" prayers are often foolishness to God. We should learn to pray, for example, that the rebellious one will be influenced by a fellow worker demonstrating true Christian love or that reading material will stimulate his or her mind to truth. Sloppy thinking in this area results in sloppy praying.

3. *Will answering my request bring glory to God?* Our mixed human motives in prayer often lead us astray. Honestly now, whose glory are we seeking? "You ask and do not receive because you ask amiss that you may spend it on your pleasures," says James.

4. *Have I done my part?* This question has often brought me to an embarrassing about-face with my own lack of adult spiritual responsibility. Often our Heavenly Parent refuses to answer certain requests because he is waiting for us to do our share, in a sense, to grow up.

When I was in the pastorate, I received a letter from a young woman who had gone out from our congregation to be a missionary in Japan. She asked us to pray that God would alleviate her loneliness. As I went to prayer, I discovered that I, her pastor, had done nothing about this need myself. Before I prayed anymore, I made sure that a regular schedule of personal letters was established, that tapes of our worship services were ordered for her, that our global community task force had a definite program of communication in mind, etc.

Then, once I had done my share, I could in good conscious pray, "Lord, our friend is lonely. Bring into her life intimate Christian fellowship. Help her to adjust to a new and bewildering culture."

5. *What is our present relationship?* The psalmist wrote, "Come and listen, all you who fear God; let me tell you what he has done for me. I cried out to him with my mouth; his praise was on my tongue. If I had cherished sin in my heart, the Lord would not have listened" (Psalm 66:16-18, NIV).

6. *Do I expect God to respond?* Well, do I really? Perhaps this is the most important question of all.

Now record your personal prayer requests. Be specific and down-to-earth in your prayers. As you write out each request, quickly evaluate it against these six questions. Add to this list as you have prayer requests in the coming days. Make sure to jot notations in the second column as you discover that your prayers are being answered.

Yes, God can be sighted as he works in our lives. We can all play I spy!

Prayer Requests   **Answers (I spy!)**

Prayer Requests   **Answers (I spy!)**

Prayer Requests   **Answers (I spy!)**

Prayer Requests

Answers (I spy!)

The God Hunt: Any time God intervenes or works in our everyday world, and we recognize it to be him.

The cumulative evidence of thirteen years of answered prayer . . . becomes weighty in its cumulative effect.

It would be next to impossible to convince me that God doesn't answer prayer. I have personal and satisfactory evidence to the contrary.

4
A MIRACLE CURE

David:

People expect miracles. According to my brother Doug, an orthopedic surgeon, that's a continuing frustration for doctors. After all, can't a doctor just give us pills to take away the fever, cure the pain, relieve the headache, and restore the faulty part? Can't Doug instantly realign the broken bone—painlessly?

We want the same miracles in our spiritual lives. But the spiritual disciplines take practice. We don't achieve sainthood overnight. We can't learn to experience the daily presence of Christ in an afternoon. However, just as there are wonder drugs for physical ills, there is a spiritual wonder drug that works miraculous cures for spiritual myopia—the inability to see the spiritual. This biblical penicillin is for us when we feel that God's in his heaven, and *nothing's* right with the world. It will help people for whom the natural world and the supernatural world never seem to meet.

That miracle drug is thanksgiving. It is a miracle cure which has rectified my spiritual nearsightedness. My prayer notebook now contains thousands of expressions of praise to the Lord—words that he rightly deserves to hear from me. Thanksgiving has opened the eyes of my soul to God.

I believe that one early indication of spiritual illness is the lack of true gratitude to God for all he has done. Paul pinpoints one of the reasons mankind is becoming so depraved: "The wrath of God is being revealed from heaven against all godlessness and wickedness of men. . . . since what may be known about God is plain to them, because God has made it plain to them. . . . For although *they knew God, they neither glorified him as God nor gave thanks to him"* (Romans 1:18-21, NIV). Show me a people who perceive that what they own or accomplish is the result of their own efforts, and I will show you a population that is becoming increasingly decadent. Show me a Christian filled with subtle pride, and I will show you an individual on the spiritual skids.

While the *neglect* of giving true thanks to God promotes ungodliness (or the inability to see God in the everyday that results in our living as though he doesn't exist), the opposite is also true. The *practice* of expressing thanks to God fosters godliness (the ability to identify his action in our world and to live in response to that reality). This is not simply a clever spiritual idea. I believe the practice of expressing appreciation to God for his goodness until it literally becomes habitual is as beneficial to the spiritually sick as a doctor-prescribed medication is for a physical ailment.

I do not know of anything in my spiritual life which has been as beneficial to me over the years as taking time almost daily to write down those items for which I want to thank my Lord.

As I look at my prayer requests, I see thanks to God for friends who mean much to me, for health, and for obvious provision for financial needs. I've written thanks for times of joy as a family, for unexpected help from someone in getting a job done, and for a special phone call or letter or word of encouragement. I have noted thanks to God for insight into a friend's problem or continuing victory in another's life.

I see where I've told the Lord I'm grateful even for a reprimand by his Spirit as well as for beautiful fellow workers, recovery from illness, or direction in a difficult decision. There are notations of thanks for answered prayer and revelation regarding scriptural passages. I've also mentioned our thankfulness for our church, for the freedom we know in America, and for the evidence of God's timing in our lives.

Consequently, I recommend that Christians take daily doses of gratefulness. Many, many Christians long for a verification of God in their everyday world—and rightly so; this is one characteristic of *normal* Christianity. Seeking God and finding him is part of the regular rhythm of Christian life. This experience of God sets us apart from the non-Christians. Many Christians do not experience *normal* Christianity, the real daily walk with God, because they don't know how to apply the prescription for spiritual health found in Scripture.

A few minutes a day is all this cure takes. I believe this disciplined practice of gratitude will work in your life like a wonder drug. I also recommend *forgiveness,* another healing force, or *confession,* a little-used but very effective curative agent. But these two medicines will flow naturally from the heart of those who have learned to thank their Heavenly Father daily.

Your Turn:
TAKING THE "THANKS MEDICINE"

David:

If the spiritual medicine I've recommended has your name on the label, take your first dose *right now.* Because the goal is to establish a habit of giving thanks, try to write your prayers of gratitude daily. Begin with this prayer: "Father, everything I record here I recognize as coming from you. My writing it down indicates my seriousness in wanting to take this cure."

Sometimes when we are suffering from lack of gratitude, we need a little help to get started. Let me give you some personal examples: *I'm thankful for food.* I'm reminded again of how many have empty stomachs while I have been given so much. You are truly good to me. *I'm thankful for peace in our land.* How much longer it will last, I don't know. But God, I thank you for this gift I experience right now.

I'm thankful for my job. I'm glad for a chance to earn a living for my loved ones by doing the kind of work I love best.

Now it's your turn. Begin to make a list of all that you are grateful for. Don't take *anything* for granted. An additional suggestion is to pray your prayers of thankfulness aloud. "Lord, I'm grateful for my spouse. Thank you for the lover and friend you have given to me." This verbal exercise is like taking a double dose of medicine!

I can almost guarantee that if you make a habit of giving thanks daily you will begin to notice surprising evidences of spiritual health. Your awareness of God's presence will be dramatically heightened. You will be well on your way to participating in the God Hunt.

Use the next few pages to record your prayers of thanksgiving.

I'm Thankful For:

april 14, 1984

I feel the beginnings of physical strength after two weeks of influenza.

Thank you for —
1. The gift of health
2. that no one else in the family caught my illness
3. household hand-me-downs from David's mother
4. The beauty of my children & the constant enjoyment they bring us.
5. The forming of a small group to meet our needs of fellowship.
6. a good church job for my brother

Thanksgiving has resulted in an overwhelming sense of God's daily presence in my life. It is the miracle cure which has rectified my spiritual nearsightedness.

5
CHARTING THE SOUL'S JOURNEY

Karen:

Insomnia has been a good friend. I owe much of my prayer life to it.

Those long, sleepless nights when we were in the pastorate worrying about the church's dissident faction; those lagging minutes before morning when the grief of a broken life or the exhausted sleep of my husband baited my soul with weight. *If day would just come!* Nighttime pain has no balm, none of the distractions that assuage waking hours.

It wasn't just pain that kept me awake. Joy could chase away slumber as well. The laughter and caffeine of a dinner party, a spiritual birth occurring right in our living room, or good conversation shot off my mental chemicals in bright, inward bursts of fireworks.

After a while, I decided that I might as well put the restless nights to useful employment. I began spraying Easy-Off in the ovens at 1:30 a.m., sorting laundry, and tearing apart messy closets. While this was wonderful for household organization, some of the seminarians who lived with us often muttered, "What on earth were you doing this morning at two?"

Scratch the time-efficient, management-effective plan. How about prayer? It was quiet and came highly recommended (and usually was boring); maybe it would put me back to sleep. About the same time I began writing my prayers down. Insomnia turned me toward prayer, but without a doubt, the discipline of keeping a prayer journal for over a decade is transforming me into a pray-before-you-do-anything-else person.

Keeping a diary of the soul's journey is not new. In past centuries, keeping a register of one's spiritual progress was regarded as part of a pious person's religious exercise.

John Wesley, for example, kept a diary for sixty-six years. His journal has been called "the most amazing record of human exertion ever penned or endured." In his diary, Wesley attributes the secret of his immense physical strength to "the good pleasure of God" which enabled him to:

"1. Constantly rise at four for about fifty years,
2. generally preach at five in the mornings: one of the most healthy exercises in the world,
3. never travel less, by sea or land, than four thousand five hundred miles in a year."

My own journal is an ongoing, daily glimpse of a soul naked before its God. For centuries, spiritual diaries have been used to record and stimulate the spiritual journey. As Elizabeth Fry, a nineteenth-century Quaker, said, "That is the advantage of a true journal. It leads the mind to look inwards."

Without a doubt, David and I agree *that of all the devotional disciplines, the journaling of prayers is the one which has most prodded our spiritual growth.*

Before beginning the discipline of keeping a prayer journal it is important (and extremely freeing) to realize that one does not have to be a literary giant to keep a diary. *Psychology Today* noted in an article, "Last year, thousands of Americans with no literary pretensions whatsoever started producing stories of surpassing interest that will probably never be published. They were writing their own, often eye-popping, tear-evoking journals, not because they felt they needed therapy, but because they wanted to put their lives in perspective and find in them some deeper meaning."*

In order to keep a prayer diary, we must also eliminate our self-consciousness. These prayer notebooks are not for any eyes but our own and God's. A prayer journal should be viewed as a workbook, a manual

---

*Robert Blair Kaiser, "The Way of the Journal," *Psychology Today* (March 1981), p. 64.

of the soul, a private testing of ourselves and our God.

My prayer journals are made up of sentence fragments, shopping lists, recipes, running columns of confessions, agonizing pleas for answered prayers, and scribbled notations in the margins. They are often illustrated with my children's art. (The notebooks have been handy to occupy a restless child on long Sunday mornings.)

Every diarist may establish his or her own unique recording mechanics. In *English Diaries,* Arthur Posonby says, "Diarists need only consult their own convenience and mood, they need obey no rules, they may follow their own inclinations to write regularly, irregularly, fully or briefly."

Some people choose a specific time of day to record. Others carry journals in their purses or glove compartments and write on the spur of the moment. David, the superorganized, goes to his prayer journal as often as three times a day, working through specific types of prayer at certain hours in a systematic fashion. I am instinctive and intuitive, attempting to stay as free-floating as possible. I work in my notebook two to three times a week. (The older I become, the more I find myself in prayer. My notebooks are records of a much broader life of prayer.)

David keeps his prayer record in a loose-leaf binder divided by topics; mine is recorded in spiral-bound notebooks. I follow the same general format each time I go to prayer, but David's notebook takes more the form of lists. Words become memory joggers between him and God. My notebook takes the form of sentences, phrases, and occasional paragraphs. Despite the differences, we both maintain rich devotional lives.

We have found several significant advantages of keeping prayer notebooks. Prayer journals encourage self-directed spiritual learning. Diarists begin to advance from the spoon-feeding necessary for baby Christians into taking more responsibility for their own spiritual growth.

Journals give their owners a concrete means of evaluating personal spiritual growth. Reviewing our prayers is important. We see where we have been, how far we have come, and where it is we must go. Because journals can be reviewed from time to time, they provide a stabilizing influence. The long view of our spiritual development helps to keep us from becoming overwhelmed by our present failures or from becoming discouraged by today's painful circumstances. We might follow the example of a man who kept a journal for many years. Each day that he wrote, he reread his entries from the corresponding date in earlier years.

Most important, a prayer notebook encourages our awareness of our unique place before God and our unique journey with him. Our consciousness of the work of the supernatural becomes heightened; we become acutely aware of the daily intervention of the Divine in our everyday lives.

In a recent experimental program, some three hundred recruits from a city's welfare and unemployment rolls participated in a journal-keeping workshop as part of their on-the-job training. The corporate profile of the group was one of repeated life failures. Ninety percent of them kept their journals over a six-month period, finished their training, and stayed on their low-status jobs. After a year, eighty percent were still on the job or had moved on to better jobs. One in three had moved on to better housing; one in four had started night school or community college.

Much of the credit for their advancement was given to the journal-keeping discipline. The director of the program stated, "Poverty is not simply the lack of money. Ultimately, it is a person's lack of feeling for the reality of his own inner being."

Spiritual poverty could be defined in much the same way. The spiritually impoverished Christian suffers from a lack of feeling for the reality of his or her inner being and the relationship of that being to God. David and I have no doubts that keeping a prayer journal is one of the quickest exits out of dead-end spirituality. It ushers us into the banquet where we feed on the fabulous spiritual riches of God.

Your Turn:
KEEPING A JOURNAL

Karen:

Individuality aside, I am aware that examples of what works for one person often stimulate ideas for another. So I have included examples from my journal here, not that you should feel bound by them, but that you'll use them as a starting point.

Often my journal begins with the *feeling prayer.* "I feel like the most loved woman in creation!" Or, "Today I feel like a big nothing!" This honest expression of feeling sets the mood for nonsanctimonious communication.

The next section is the *God Hunt* (anytime God intervenes in our lives, and we recognize it to be him). For me, this most frequently begins "I thank you for . . .", followed by a list of items. I am constantly amazed by how much I discover the supernatural in the everyday of my life and how proportionate this discovery is to my gratitude.

I rarely move on without a *forgiveness and confession check*. Do I need to forgive anyone who has intentionally or unintentionally wounded me? Do I need to confess and receive forgiveness because I am the one who stands in error? (Yes, I write these out. David keeps his in code!) This cleansing keeps my soul free from disease and enables me to approach my heavenly Papa with intimacy.

At this point, I choose one attribute of God for the purpose of *adoration*. Sometimes it helps me to think of adoring God in terms of paying him a compliment. In other words I say, "This is what I really like about you."

I might begin by praising him that he is love. The adoration would continue: "I praise you that your love is not manipulative like much human love. It is a steadfast love, without treachery or guile. Your love is not partial. It does not play favorites. It does not exclude the unlovely. It is sacrificial and, at the same time, tough. Your love is the demonstration for how we are to love. Without your love shed abroad in the world, we would have no idea what true love is."

Sometimes I allow my creative abilities to weave new names and to retell the old ones in a new way: "You are the Spring-Maker who dresses the world in green, and you are the one who whispers *spring! spring! spring!* to each brown-seared winter soul. I praise you, fresh God." Amazingly, I never run out of names.

This adoration helps to raise our consciousness regarding God's nature. The more we discover the infinite variety of his nature, the more we develop our ability to recognize that nature at work in the world.

Next comes a section of *debriefing prayers*. Here I dump all the nitty-gritty concerns that clog my existence. Usually this section is headed, "I need your help, God, with . . . ", and I am embarrassed to admit that it is often the longest. "Help, God, with the broadcast due next Monday, to get decent meals on the table, to organize my hectic schedule." (The column by these prayers is also filled with notations of prayers answered—proof positive to me of God's overwhelming work in my daily life.)

It is only after I have cleared my heart of these items that I can begin to work at the prayer that is hardest for me, *intercession*. Here I hold up the world or nations or individuals before the mind of God so that in some mysterious fashion his will can be worked in them. I begin by saying, "Lord, how would you have me pray for this my brother (or this national or international situation)?" Sometimes my concerns are personal, as for the health of a friend. Sometimes they are international or cosmic, such as protection from nuclear confrontation or the preparation of the world for the coming again of Christ.

The last section is the *prayer of listening*. "What is it you have to say to me, Lord?" This is the time for silence, a deliberately disciplining of my soul to be still. I cease talking and wait, ready to receive. I write down all thoughts that come to my mind. Sometimes I find that they have really been God's whispers. Even when I don't hear that inward word, this exercise in silence prepares me to be listening when the world around me is full of noise.

The following pages will help you get started in the devotional discipline of keeping a prayer journal. I have included the headings I feel comfortable working with. Fill them in from your personal experience as a prayer notebook exercise. Maybe they will stimulate some recording ideas that are uniquely your own.

The Feeling Prayer

Write out an answer to your heavenly Father's question, "Child, how are you feeling today?" Use descriptive words or phrases.

The God Hunt

You have worked with this category in earlier chapters, but practice makes perfect. Head this section "I Spy" or begin with the phrase "I thank you for . . ." Now make a list beneath your headings.

The Forgiveness and Confession Check

Divide this section into two parts, "I forgive" and "I confess." Make a list under each heading.

The Prayer of Adoration

Praise (or adoration) can be thought of as paying compliments to God. There is a fine line between praise and thanksgiving. Thanksgiving focuses on something God has done for you. Praise is more likely to focus on a characteristic of God's nature (although it has consequent bearing on our relationship with him and the world around us). Choose one attribute of God's and praise God for all that relates to this attribute. Write these thoughts out in sentences or brief phrases.

Debriefing Prayers

Which areas in your life need divine intervention? Be specific, and don't be afraid to bring the minute concerns of your everyday existence to your heavenly Father. He is not too busy to take interest in the mundane aspects of your life. In fact, it is in these minor, but troublesome, areas he most frequently demonstrates his love. Faith is built in the trivial so that we can trust God to take care of the areas of overwhelming magnitude. Begin this section, "Lord, I need your help with . . ." List words or phrases beneath it.

The Prayer of Intercession
What are you burdened about? Is it personal? national? cosmic? Begin by asking, "Lord, how would you have me pray?" Write your requests and any thoughts that come to your mind as you pray.

The Prayer of Listening

Many people today are not skilled at cultivating silence. The prayer of listening is one way to develop this skill. If you are a novice at using silence creatively, begin by remaining quiet for a few minutes and then increase your capacity as you see fit. (Begin with two minutes, slowly increasing it to ten.) This is silence for the sake of hearing the inward voice of God. Remind yourself that you are in his presence. (You may want to use your imagination to see the form of Christ.) When your mind wanders, gently bring it back to an attitude of listening to God for the determined amount of time. If you have any ideas, if you recall Scripture, or if you have any thoughts about actions to accomplish or to cease from accomplishing, write these down. You never know what you will hear. You might begin with the following prayer: "Lord, I am listening to you. I have said enough. Now if there is anything you have to say to me, I am ready to hear."

"The journal is a place where tender new growth is privately and secretly nourished, away from the burning eyes and the blasting voices of others. It is the hidden chamber where awkward new steps can be practiced until we are sure enough to take them out into everyday life. . . . It is an ongoing book which will be a continuing response to the nagging question—'Who am I?'"

George F. Simons
Keeping Your Own Personal Journal

6
WITCHES' KNOTS

Karen:

I delight in giving gifts to my children. However, my family suspected that the horse I bought for my daughter's sixteenth birthday was not really for Melissa, but for myself. I suspect they were right!

Melissa bore the brunt of the responsibility—feeding Lady Sundown and mucking out the stall—and received most of the pleasure—taking long rides near the small farm where we boarded the horse. But I, too, grabbed stolen moments for relaxing rides, and I found myself filling in as stable hand at times when my daughter's schedule became prohibitive.

There is nothing quite like a cold barn on a winter day with hoarfrost on the ground and the warm breath of a welcoming animal blowing clouds of vapor. I loved a reckless gallop along the edge of a cornfield or walking down a sweaty horse by way of the orchard and swiping late apples from the trees.

Yet to everything there is a season. When Melissa left for college, I faced the inevitable and found some potential buyers for a first-class horse. Believe me, this was not an easy decision; one becomes emotionally bonded to fulfilled longings!

I set aside one morning to groom Lady Sundown so she would look her best at my private horse sale. Much to my dismay, I found that she had escaped to the front pasture which had gone to weed. Sundown's mane was a maze of tangles impossibly matted together with briars and stickers.

My first impulse was to take scissors and cut out the tangles because I knew it would take hours to comb through the knots. I'm not much of a horsewoman, but I had been told that this particular shortcut is forbidden. One spreads the tangles and patiently combs them smooth. Better yet, a responsible owner never allows her horse to get in such a state.

So I resigned myself to a long morning, led my horse into the barn, and fastened her halter to the chains above the grooming floor. I brushed the summer dust from her mahogany coat, dug the mud from her hooves with a shoe pick, and finally tackled the dread mess of her mane. I had been right; it took me two hours to spread the knots, spray them with untangling solution, then comb them smooth.

Appropriately, these tangles in a horse's mane are called witches' knots. Folklore says that witches, out of love for chaos and pure spitefulness, tie these time-consuming masses. That morning, I could almost believe there was some evil design behind my tedious work.

Eventually I finished and saddled Lady Sundown for one last ride. Standing aside, I admired the results of my morning's frustrating work. A groomed horse whose brushed and polished flanks shine in the sun is beautiful.

I was glad I hadn't chopped away the tangles. There would have been no way to hide the hacked hair; my impatience would have maimed the beauty I had always loved.

Life is also full of witches' knots where the twisted circumstances of living and relationships seem impossible to untie. How many times I have found myself thinking, *There is no end to this dilemma.* All I have wanted to do is cut away the knot of impossibilities.

In her little book, *IF,* Amy Carmichael has described me rather well: "IF I wonder why something trying is allowed, and press for prayer that it may be removed; if I cannot be trusted with any disappointment, and cannot go on in peace under any mystery, then I know nothing of Calvary love.

"IF I ask to be delivered from trial rather than for deliverance out of it;

. . . if I forget that the way of the Cross leads to the Cross and not to a bank of flowers . . . so that I am surprised when the way is rough and think it strange, though the word is, *Think it not strange, Count it all joy,* then I know nothing of Calvary love."

I have been a master of praying for God to change my difficult circumstances. Only recently have I learned how to pray for God to change me in the midst of the difficult circumstances. I have found myself approaching the witches' knots of my life with an unusual kind of patience. I have found myself determining to comb through the tangles rather than to cut them out. What is the basic reason for this attitude shift? Daily identifying God in the ordinary events of life has enabled me to see his presence in the midst of the pain-filled extraordinary circumstances that sooner or later we all face.

Consequently, I am convinced that the God Hunt stabilizes us to cope when we find our lives in knots bound so tight we think we will never be free.

Grief sits heavy on our chests. Death lifts a jeering face at us and smirks. Rejection nags us, isolation taunts us, rebellion mocks us. And at these moments when our heads pound from stress, our hearts feel about to burst, and self-disgust threatens to overwhelm us, then we remember another old, sweet melody, "But God . . . but God . . . but God . . ."

We open our prayer journals and recall the times when we made Sightings. The many, many notations beside the columns of prayer requests stand as evidence. We remember how God surprised us with intimacy, whispering "boo!" when we had lost our way. We find that the lists of thanks recorded over years are healing balm to our battered souls. We are not abandoned; he does not delight in our torture.

Then we are given strength to comb through our tangled circumstances instead of maiming our growth by cutting out of them. Because we have developed the habit of looking for God daily, his presence suddenly overwhelms us when our own resources are depleted and when we are suffering from the poison of the Viper's bite.

The Apostle Paul writes: "The truth is that, although we lead normal human lives, the battle we are fighting is on the spiritual level. The very weapons we use are not human but powerful in God's warfare for the destruction of the enemy's strongholds. Our battle is to break down every deceptive argument and every imposing defence that men erect against the true knowledge of God. We fight to capture every thought until it acknowledges the authority of Christ" (II Corinthians 10:3-5, Phillips).

One way to "capture every thought until it acknowledges the authority of Christ" is to train our minds to see God in the everyday, identifying his activity in our ordinary world. The God Hunt is one of the powerful weapons in spiritual warfare that brings about the destruction of the enemy's strongholds. If we have been practicing it on an everyday level, it will become a shield and a defense when we are in the middle of bloody spiritual conflict.

Your Turn:
GOING ON THE GOD HUNT

David:

We must understand that the God Hunt is not a spiritual charade. We are not acting out the title of God's drama in the world to one another. Through the God Hunt we are participating in the drama of God with us.

We don't fabricate the God Hunt. God is not in need of super-hype public relations agents who puff his cause in the world. No, finding God is a real event; we report on what actually is, and we must learn not to become immune to his Real Presence in our everyday lives, to begin to take the supernatural for granted and to manipulate it for our own ends. How many men and women have known the Presence, have experienced its powerful reality, only to begin to build their own kingdoms and have become like King Saul, where the Spirit departed from him and he knew it not.

Witches' knots are often allowed in our lives so that God can work that painful crucifixion of the self in us that keeps us building his Kingdom and not our own. It is this work of the cross within each human heart, this breaking of our self-will, our self-arrogance, our latent spirit of rebellion which we must each experience if we are to become truly like Christ.

The God Hunt will prepare us to learn to identify the miracle of his Presence in each commonplace moment so that when times of personal crucifixion occur, we will most assuredly know that he stands at the foot of each man's cross, that he allows suffering so we will better identify with a suffering world.

Only then, in moments of extreme pain, do we see the true beauty of the supernatural, that he is with us in our distress. We can discover the great I Am of this terrible moment (as well as the I Am of the moments of joy or ordinariness). One of the greatest fruits of the discipline of the God Hunt is the discovery that *he is* no matter our circumstances, and that in him, so can we be.

Now begin the God Hunt in earnest. Contract with yourself to look for God in your everyday world. Fill out the following agreement, decide on the amount of time you will need to develop this spiritual discipline, and then begin to record the incidents of divine Sightings in this notebook.

Remember, there is no need to fabricate God's work in the world. His reputation is not dependent on how many times you sight his work; nor is the level of your spirituality to be measured by the ease or frequency of these Sightings. Simply record the evidences which you suspect might be indications of his Presence. In a sense, this is a spiritual experiment. Your life is the laboratory in which you are seeking him.

There will be a cumulative effect, however. If you are faithful in recording the God Hunt, you will begin to experience a heightened sensitivity to God's Presence. The daily record will begin to speak volumes to your own soul that God is there, that he is working in your life, and that he loves you.

> I agree to deliberately watch for God in my everyday world for (time period). I will record these Sightings in this notebook for that amount of time. As I record these suspected evidences of God, I will also take a moment to determine into which of the four categories these personal glimpses of God fall.
> Signed: _____
> Date: _____

THE GOD HUNT
Categories:
1. Any obvious answer to prayer.
2. Any unexpected evidence of God's care.
3. Any unusual linkage or timing.
4. Any help to do God's work in the world.

Date: **Sighting:**   **Category:**

Date:　　　　　　**Sighting:**　　　　　　**Category:**

Date: **Sighting:** **Category:**

Date: **Sighting:** **Category:**

"IF the love that 'alone maketh light of every heady thing, and beareth evenly every uneven thing' is not my heart's desire, then I know nothing of Calvary love."

Amy Carmichael
IF

"Daily identifying God in the ordinary events of life has enabled me to see his Presence in the midst of the pain-filled extraordinary circumstances that sooner or later we all face."

7
BRING THE CHILDREN ALONG

David:

Many families find it impossible to talk about spiritual matters. What better way to begin than to introduce this marvelous God Hunt game which reaps such positive spiritual results? The God Hunt makes it easy to communicate about God's work without weighty theological terminology. Our children, as well as adults who happen into our lives, find it fascinating to share how God has surprised them with his activity in our everyday lives. "I had an 'I spy' today" is simple to say.

Every few Saturdays, the Mains family gathers together to prepare our hearts to worship the next morning. At this time, we make a practice of sharing the God Hunt. We record our Sightings in a family God Hunt notebook. This is an ongoing record of God's work in our lives, a personal testament to the ways we have identified him. Often extended family is present. Think of the beauty for a small child to hear his uncles or aunts share how they have identified God. Think of the spiritual reinforcement when a small child hears a parent or an older sibling report on an "I spy." A child accustomed to this atmosphere begins to assume that it is natural to the Christian life to see God at work in the world.

When our older children come home from college they often ask, "When are we going to share the God Hunt?" Even young children can play the game. Our nephews, one a preschooler and the other in grade school, feel at ease with this vocabulary and regularly share new "I spys" with us.

As Christ taught, our language is truly indicative of the condition of the heart. I can think of no better way to begin to teach children to be comfortable speaking about God's involvement in the world, than by introducing them to the God Hunt.

We begin early to point out the activity of God in our children's lives: "Don't you remember that you prayed for a friend? Now you have two new friends, the boy who moved in down the block and the Christian boy you discovered in your class. God has answered your prayers. That's an 'I spy.' "

The role of the Christian parent is to point out God to his or her children. It is we who cry "Sighting!" in order to teach them how to identify the supernatural in the Christian's life. But if we are not identifying him in our lives, we will be unable to teach our children how to do so.

Karen and I have never been very successful at family devotions, if by "family devotions" one is referring to an authoritarian *paterfamilias* gathering his eager and well-behaved offspring around the open Bible and reading to them a chapter a day (genealogies included). I have always admired those who have been able to establish this form of family discipline, but it never seemed to work for our clan.

I am not saying that we have failed teaching our children scriptural truth. But by the nature of our family personality and structure, we have been forced to discover creative approaches for our teaching. The God Hunt is just one of these.

Our teaching of spiritual truth begins with the conviciton that the family has the major responsibility for this teaching. This is too important a job to be delegated to just forty-five minutes of Sunday school or to a weekly Bible club. The best spiritual training must be *organic*—truth applied to the child's everyday needs—and only a parent on the spot is aware of a child's daily life.

In fact, scriptural truth over the long haul without personal life application is dangerous. The child (as well as the adult) begins to assume that the spiritual world and the everyday world do not mix. To avoid this, Karen and I have attempted to fit the truth to the child's need and interest. Some spiritual training is like the one-size-fits-all glove. More frequently, different ages need different sizes—an infant needs mittens (with strings to prevent their being lost), older children need waterproof protection against the rough and tumble of outdoor play, and adults are more able to take proper care of leather, fur-lined gloves.

Together, Karen and I analyze our children's emotional, physical, social, and spiritual development. Is the child developing in the interest areas that we feel are unique to the child? How can we as parents introduce the child to learning environments that will enhance these interest areas? Does the child need to participate in a sport, maybe one that he or she can enjoy during the adult years? Does the child have the right kind of friends? Can we invite a neighbor child whose friendship we encourage to join us on a family weekend outing? Is our child struggling with academics? If so, how can we create homelife that will be more conducive to study?

I am well aware that this parental executive committee is an ideal. Where there is death, divorce, physical absence, or emotional distance, a single parent can invite the input of other adults who are interested in the child's development: grandparent, teacher, or church child worker.

For a parent already coping with an anxiety-producing marital breakdown, outside evaluation can be viewed as another threatening situation (someone is going to tell me what I am doing wrong with my kids). But there is strength in the counsel of many, a concept the Book of Proverbs emphasizes on numerous occasions. Take courage and seek out those people who are interested in or love your children. Ask them to serve as an unofficial committee for the purpose of evaluation.

The evaluation session can healthily be conducted with the child present—"Mom and Dad know it is terrible to be lonely. You tell us why you think you don't have any friends. Maybe there are some ways we can work together to solve this problem." Afterwards, Karen and I divide the responsibility. For instance, my wife is good at providing reading material that she feels will intrigue each child. She follows the day-to-day activities a little better than I do and keeps me informed, but I love to schedule and organize special family outings. Karen is more spontaneous in regard to the children's needs, whereas I am better at the long-range planning that she hates.

We have worked together at discovering how we can best team in the parenting of our four children, using each other's strengths and covering each other's weaknesses.

When evaluating each child's spiritual growth, we ask: Where is the living edge of that child's spiritual interest?

This has meant my holding a teen accountable as he and I undertook a mutual study of the Book of Amos. It has meant reading the *Chronicles of Narnia* at bedtime. It has meant faithfully sharing in one of the children's prayer concerns. It has meant discussing Sunday morning sermons in the car after church. It has meant including unsaved playmates in family activities, saving money to send the children on overseas missionary projects so they would see the work of God worldwide, and inviting into our home Christians with testimonies of God's work in their lives.

Our experience with Joel, our high schooler, will illustrate what we try to do with all the children. Joel has a strong interest in contemporary Christian music. Instead of fighting this, we have chosen to run with his special interest area.

We've helped Joel purchase a stereo so he could collect the records and cassettes he enjoys. We've provided guitar lessons, and subscribed to *Contemporary Christian Music* magazine. We've introduced Joel to friends in the Christian music industry. We've held thorough discussions regarding entertainment versus ministry, developing the ability to evaluate, and being cautious about personality cults.

While contempory Christian music is not a strong interest area of Karen's or mine, we have seen it bring spiritual benefit to Joel's life. He has used this interest to integrate the spiritual with his life in a public high school. Listening to records with non-Christian friends has provided an opportunity for Joel to explain the meaning of lyrics that have excellent scriptual messages.

Christian music has been integrated into speeches for English class as well as a recent school video project. Joel and a friend supply contemporary Christian cassettes for the library at school and view this as a mission outreach. Through all of this, Joel has developed a broader interest in music and now participates in two student choirs and is trying out for a school musical.

This is what we mean by training a child's spiritual growth *organically.* The correct spiritual glove is fitted to the correct spiritual size. As we are alert to the teachable moment, we become adept at this type of spiritual training in children of all ages. The teachable moment is that time when the *child* indicates a spiritual receptivity. It is the question asked at the most inopportune moment, "Mom, why does God love bad people?" It's the eager face at the end of a long, hard day, "Daddy, read me a Bible story, please."

These are the moments the astute parent grabs. As much as possible, we learn to put aside our fatigue of adult agendas and take time for spiritual cultivation at the moments when the child himself indicates interest. This kind of spiritual training is scriptural. Deuteronomy 6:6, 7 says, "These commandments that I give you today are to be upon your hearts. Impress them on your children. Talk about them when you sit at home and when you walk along the road, when you lie down and when you get up" (NIV).

Organic spiritual training has demanded that I be constantly on my own spiritual toes. If I am not growing spiritually, my children will know it. I have no business demanding growth of them if I am not demanding it of myself. It is an awesome spiritual responsibility to be a parent.

Using the teachable moment and the child's spiritual receptivity along with the God Hunt works well for our family. It makes our pursuit of God a delight.

The God Hunt makes it easy for families to talk about the spiritual, but it also raises our consciousness as a *family* about the intimacy of God's Presence. It enables us to talk about intimate concerns in a nonthreatening way. It is a safeguard against becoming a secularized Christian family.

So begin with the delightful chase—and take your children along with you.

Your Turn:
TRAINING THE CHILDREN

Record when you will share the God Hunt with your children.

Sightings We've Made As a Family

Sightings We've Made As a Family

Sightings We've Made As a Family

Sightings We've Made As a Family

"The teachable moment is that time when the child indicates a spiritual receptivity. . . . These are the moments the astute parent grabs."

"The role of the Christian parent is to point out God to his or her children."

In addition to the family God Hunt, older children and teens will want to keep individual God Hunt journals. The companion notebooks, *The God Hunt: A Discovery Book for Boys and Girls* and *The God Hunt: A Discovery Book for Teens* will help them begin the lifelong hunt.